POEMS THAT MATTER

Book 1

A Look at Common life in

an Uncommon World!

John Holt

Published by:

MaxHoltMedia

John Holt   Poems That Matter – Book One

POEMS THAT MATTER – BOOK 1
© 2020 John Holt

All rights reserved. No part of this book may be reproduced in any form or by any means, without written permission by the publisher, except by a reviewer who may quote brief passages in a review.

Published by MaxHoltMedia
303 Cascabel Place, Mount Juliet, TN 37122
www.maxholtmedia.com

The author is totally responsible for the content and the editing of this work and Max Holt Media offers no warranty, expressed or implied, or assumes any legal liability or responsibility for the accuracy of any information contained herein. The author bears responsibility for obtaining permission to use any portion of this work that may be the intellectual property of another person or organization.

Cover design by: Max Holt Media
ISBN-13: 978-1-944537-39-5

John Holt					Poems That Matter – Book One

	CONTENTS	Page
	Author's Notes	8
	Dedication	10
	Foreword	12
1.	Wasted Life	14
2.	Klausen And Boone	14
3.	Defrauded	15
4.	I'd Rather Draw the Blueprints	16
5.	Impossible Things	18
6.	Laughter	20
7.	The Sour Man	22
8.	Destiny	23
9.	The Manipulator	24
10.	The Parasite	25
11.	The Dictator	26
12.	Raindrops	27
13.	The Skeptic And The Feather	28
14.	Bringing Home The Bacon	29
15.	Watching The Clock	30
16.	A Gentle June Rain	31
17.	Spring Shelter	32
18.	The Parachutist	32
19.	Sunshine for The Children	33
20.	Busy	34
21.	Worry	34
22.	Ode To The Stone Caster	35
23.	Eternal Worth	35
24.	Why Do We Do It?	36
25.	Family Reunion Memories	37
26.	The Land Of Fantasy	38
27.	Ode to The Fisherman	39
28.	The Lonely Man of Contention	40
29.	The Daily Fray	42
30.	Procrastination	43
31.	The Brutish Man	44
32.	Afterglow of A Hug	45
33.	Shout Is Clout to The Dumb	46

34. Approval	46
35. Funny Barnyard Scene	47
36. Autonomy	47
37. Farewell To The Lazy	48
38. Simple Gifts	48
39. Beauty	49
40. Lacing My Shoes	50
41. The Kids Are Gone, But----	51
42. The Make Up of The Day	52
43. Mining The Heart	53
44. Daddies	54
45. The Optimist	55
46. The End Is the Beginning	56
47. Ode to The Cook	57
48. Bad Apples	58
49. Letting Go	59
50. Old Parents	60
51. Small Men	60
52. Hug Me!	60
53. Loyalty	61
54. Situational Ethics	61
55. As A Man Thinketh	62
56. Reaching Higher	63
57. Springtime in Texas	64
58. Time Passes So Fast	64
59. The Fat Man	65
60. How To Succeed	65
61. Look Beyond the Trees	66
62. The Purpose Of A Poem	67
63. Sunshine For The Heart	68
64. The Heart Song	69
65. Growing Up	70
66. A Hug Would Make My Day	70
67. The Land Of Lying	71
68. Success	72
69. A Candle	73
70. Ode to The Omelet Maker	74

71. The Fool and The Fireplace	74
72. The Toothpick	75
73. The Butterfly	75
74. I Wear A Smile	76
75. In A Tizzy	77
76. The Mongrel Millionaire	78
77. Wretched	79
78. Disadvantage is Advantage	80
79. Don't Sweat the Small Stuff	81
80. Again!	81
81. If You Faint in The Day of Adversity	82
82. The Bond of The Heart	83
83. Rowing Against the Tide	84
84. The Life House	85
85. False Guilt	85
86. Good Medicine	86
87. Deadly Faults	87
88. Secluded Island	88
89. Death of A Snowflake	90
90. Old Mose	90
91. Irritation	91
92. The Mantle of The Day	92
93. Talk Is Cheap	93
94. A Philosophical View of Things	94
95. You Never Will Know	95
96. The Athlete Lee	95
97. The All-American Pig	96
98. The Anvil	97
99. Robin Hood	98
101. My Guinea Pig Ted	99
102. The Security of The Familiar	99
103. Thinker	100
104. Urgency of Goals	100
105. Pearls Before Swine	101
106. To lighten up the Load	101
107. As the Child Is Bent	102
108. Essie and Effie	103
109. If You Will Try	104

110. The Pioneer Man	105
111. Heartaches	105
112. The Diamond	106
113. Faith and Intellect	108
114. Ode to Ego	109
115. The Shortest Way Home	110
116. Never Give Gifts	111
117. The Uncommon Common Man	112
118. God Set A Time	112
119. The Obviation of Buford Jones	113
120. Rejection	113
121. One Small Rose	114
122. Ode to The Poet Carpenter	115
123. The Pendulum Swings Where It's Been	116
124. An Organized Mind	118
125. Home	119
126. The Wordsmith	119
127. An Inch of Time	120
128. Time II	121
129. Water Seeks Its Level	121
130. Habits	122
131. The Unknown Trail	123
132. Significance	124
133. Materialism	125
134. This Newfangled Electronic Age	126
135. The Animal Trainer	128
136. A Well Spent Yesterday	129
137. The Good Old Days	130
138. The Dour Gang	132
139. The Winepress	133
140. Redneck	134
141. Contemplation	135
142. Beggar or Boss	136
143. The Candle	138
144. Weffa	139
About the Author	140
Poem Titles – Alphabetical	142
Poem First Lines – Alphabetical	144

AUTHOR'S NOTES

I don't remember when I first became a poet. I wrote poems to my girlfriend when I was in fifth grade. I am glad none of them are available now. I remember reading poetry in high school English classes and was amazed how someone could say things in rhyme and have it come out even at the end of the sentence.

I was encouraged by Grace Brandenburg, my Senior English teacher. She saw then what I did not see until much later. Most high school boys played sports and left poetry and music to the girls.

I discovered I was thinking rhyme through the day. I looked at cars, birds, and endless people situations and thought of rhyme as I mentally described all that I saw. I received inspiration from hearing speakers use poems to make a point or ministers use poetry to close a thought in an inspiring way.

At the risk of sounding egotistical, I do not write poems; it is that I can't *help* writing poems. It is no effort to write and it is relaxing to put my thoughts into rhyme.

I do not try to copy those poets regarded as the great examples of rhyme or regarded by the literary world as the *great ones*. I do not attempt to compete in that league. I just write about common people and common things as I see them.

If you find a poem somewhere in this book that lifts and encourages you, then it has been worth all the work it has taken to publish it. The CONTENTS page lists the poems in the order I prefer to present them. You will also find a list of the poem titles in Alphabetical order starting on page 142. A list of poems by first lines follows on page 144.

John Holt - Delaware, Ohio

John Holt   Poems That Matter – Book One

DEDICATION

I want to dedicate this book of poems to Jesus Christ, my Lord and Savior. He gave me the gift of poetry, and the opportunity to publish them. I pray He will receive any glory that may result from their publication.

To my sweetheart wife of 58 years, Lon Nell. She has read many of my poems and offered helpful insights and suggestions I did not think of or see. She is mother to our three children, loving grandmother and great grandmother. To my fellow poem addict and a source of inspiration, my nephew Walter Adams. To my family members and many friends who have read my poems and encouraged me to publish them.

Finally, to my publisher and brother, Max Holt. He has encouraged me to put my thoughts and experiences of life on paper. He has given me this opportunity to publish and I will ever be grateful and do my best to be worthy of his herculean efforts and generous time spent to put my literary thought before the public.

John Holt   Poems That Matter – Book One

FOREWORD

One could see the gift in John in his childhood years. He was musically inclined and when grown, he honed his God-given talent with educational training. He then served many decades in Christian music ministry, where God used his talent and expertise to touch many lives.

Later in life, another talent was revealed as John began writing poetry. At times, expressions came flowing out in unexpected, refreshing ways so he could hardly write fast enough to capture them. In all styles and categories, you will find John's poems interesting. My favorites change with moods; at the present time I frequently enjoy reading, **"If I Could See."** It moves me each time I read it.

As a published author of devotional books, I know what a task it is to get your writings ready for publication. John has done the difficult work of sorting, compiling, and editing his poems so that others can also enjoy them.

I encourage you to share John's gift with others around you. They will be encouraged and will be grateful for your thoughtfulness.

Edna Holmes
Bonham, Texas

John Holt					Poems That Matter – Book One

Wasted Life

If we gathered up the minutes
We have wasted living life,
And measured them in days and years,
We could have lived it twice.

J Holt 2-10-2013

Klausen And Boone

Klausen and Boone were railroad men,
Both worked for the Santa Fe,
Klausen worked for the railroad,
Boone worked for the pay.

All day long Boone watched the clock
Begrudging all his time,
Klausen watched the Sante Fe,
And all its railroad lines.

Retirement time on the railroad,
Each man said good-by,
Klausen rides free on the railroad,
Boone watches the trains go by.

J Holt 12-8-96

Defrauded

I saw a poor man near the street,
A cardboard sign in hand,
The cold rain blurred the words he wrote,
But I could understand.

The warm fire dried his clothing,
As we drank coffee he talked,
He seemed ill fitted for begging,
Why now the path he walked?

His speech belied deeper thinking
Than most who lived like this,
Had Providence been thus unkind,
Some opportune he missed?

He had been defrauded,
Not fate, or friend, or brother,
He rowed his boat of life one way,
While looking to another.

J Holt 11-26-10

I'd Rather Draw the Blueprints

I'd rather draw the blueprints
than I had to lay the bricks,
Design the clocks and watches
than I had to make them tick,
I'd rather make the music and
let others hear the song,
Write the laws rather than
enforce the right and wrong.

I'd rather live each moment
than to sleep my life away,
And always be so diligent
I'd never waste a day,
I'd rather have integrity
so deep and so ingrained,
That every day I gather,
from the fields of golden grain.

I'd rather have God's rightest blessings
measured to me full,
And know His hidden secrets which
He hides from doubting fools,
Opportune will come and knock
each morning at the door,
Bidding every man believe
and try again once more.

I'd rather say I've done one thing,
Just something simple wrought,
And leave behind me someone helped
because of what I taught,
The oak sleeps in the acorn and
but needs to germinate,
But it must use the season,
Time won't hesitate.

The thinking man will live
his life on higher, fairer plains,
Than one confined by habits which
forbid him using brains,
Nothing more excites a man
than breathing virgin air,
It's worth the climb every time,
to be the first one there.

J Holt 9-26-95

Impossible Things

You cannot drink yourself sober,
Nor borrow yourself out of debt,
You cannot wish yourself wealthy,
Nor prosper yourself on a bet.

You can't overcome without effort,
Nor build without a good plan,
You cannot make others happy,
Nor, doubt, and still understand.

You cannot make friends without loving,
Nor maintain the truth with a lie,
You cannot lose weight overeating,
Nor wish bad habits to die.

You cannot learn prayer without praying,
Nor learn to swim on the shore,
You cannot eat free without working,
Nor pass through the walls without doors.

You cannot escape from your shadow,
Nor buy integrity,
You cannot give without getting,
You cannot make honey like bees.

You cannot mix goodness and evil,
Nor dry up the ocean with drought,
You can't run a railroad with one rail,
Nor confirm your convictions with doubt.

You can't love and hate the same person,
Nor savor success without trials,
You cannot pretend you're committed,
Nor get there and not go the miles.

You can't give success to a sluggard,
You can't make a foolish man think,
You cannot embolden a coward,
Nor be a good scribe without ink.

God made the rules that govern,
He only can set them aside,
A man is a fool to circumvent rules,
And wise to let them abide.

J Holt 3-31-98

Laughter

I've laughed away a ton of care
And sweetened simple life,
And cheerfulness has walked with me,
When my place had no spice.

I've been humiliated and
I've been depressed and sad,
But looking back and laughing now,
It wasn't all that bad.

A laugh outweighs a hundred groans,
It makes us all forget,
It gives us transient pleasures,
And nullifies regret.

A chuckle 'neath the buckle
Will improve one's frame of mind,
It's sunshine in the dungeon
In the most depressing time.

I've not been the king of day,
Nor foreman of the night,
I've had the happiest heart 'ere beat,
I've laughed with all my might.

I've not hung my name up high
For all the world to see,
Of all the mortals here on earth,
There's none so glad as me.

J Holt 10-27-95

The Sour Man

He yelled and screamed and yet it seemed
That nothing I could do,
Would satisfy the lad who cried,
For he was only two.

He shouted and he pouted for,
He felt his friends untrue,
For none could feed the ego
Of the lad at twenty-two.

He blamed his wife and blamed his kids,
For things he could not do,
He said he gave but none re-payed,
When he was forty-two.

He sat and sulked and cursed his luck,
And said he'd paid his "due,"
And none could lift his spirit,
When he was sixty-two.

He wore a constant frown and still
Complained his whole life through,
He lived 'til he was eighty,
But he died at twenty-two.

J Holt 11-15-92

Destiny

On distant plains of destiny,
Awaiting every man,
The just rewards that Life will pay,
For every deed and plan.

We take the threads Life in hand,
Weave purpose or neglect,
Though memory fade, yet Providence
Will surely resurrect.

Man may choose the day at hand,
Or chance of the unknown,
But surely as the sun will rise,
We reap as we have sown.

J Holt 3-14-10

The Manipulator

At first his words were soft and meek,
"It's just a bit of food I seek,"
Many would respond with coin or bill,
T'was plain to see his awful plight,
His brightest day had turned to night,
Seldom did he eat a wholesome meal.

I did not think his time would last,
He learned the minds of those who passed,
He turned from begging to manipulate,
I thought my meager giving
Was the sole source of his living,
And so my guilty conscience to sedate.

When he disappeared from sight,
To inquire why it would be right,
I found his home in neighborhood "success,"
I rang the bell and spoke his name,
She seemed surprised to see I came,
"He's sitting in the parlor playing chess."

J Holt 5-16-08

The Parasite

The soft touch of my tendrils is subtle, a caress,
Disarming to your hospitality,
Scarcely is my presence felt when I attach myself,
To burrow in unperceptively.

I cast no shadow to alarm, I have no silhouette,
I have no heart to give myself a form,
I rob you of identity and live your life until,'
You're too weak to keep me from my harm.

I'll restrict your breathing and make you suffocate,
I'll let you plan your day and there I'll live,
I'll bully in when you have dreamed your dreams,
And pillage them expecting you'll forgive.

I have no life to call my own, so I will live in yours,
Demanding more as I grow strong each hour,
I'll rob you of your hopes and dreams and love,
Replacing them with mine when I have power.

J Holt 9-21-98

The Dictator

I will make all your decisions,
Forbid you to ever think,
I'll beat you down and then with a frown,
Scold you when you finally sink.

I'll scorn you for not making choices,
And change the ones that you do,
Give guilt to each breath you take in your chest,
And slowly rob you, of you.

The things I stop you from saying
Will change the way you behave,
When you receive the things I believe,
Unknowing, you'll be my slave.

Sooner or later Dictator will die,
And you will have freedom alone,
You will not play host to this wretched ghost,
And finally, you'll be on your own.

J Holt 7-15-08

Raindrops

Raindrops ever falling ever dropping are appalling,
But they only wet the clothes and wet the skin,
No shelter from the storm of daily present scorn,
Will chill you to the bone deep within.

No one has the power it takes to stop a shower,
There's shelter from the roof when you are home,
Nothing's as defeating if the spirit gets a beating
Of rejecting scorn that soaks you to the bone.

J Holt 5-27-91

The Skeptic And The Feather

A skeptic thought a feather was as heavy as a brick,
Thinking people also thought the silly skeptic sick,
People of reality would laugh at such a sham,
Except other skeptics thinking just like him.

Other skeptics talked about their own bricks and feathers
Challenging officially accepted weights and measures,
Common sense had said a pound always weighs a pound,
The skeptics said refuting evidence had been found.

No one thought insanity as this could change the law,
T'il well-fed other skeptics joined the skeptic's thought,
If public platform gives a voice to skeptics and to fools,
Nations are destroyed if truth is not the rule.

The skeptics thought themselves normal of IQ,
And swore truthful scales weighed the feather true,
No one saw the unseen ones who gave the skeptics vent,
But knew of sure destruction when the truth of life is bent.

J Holt 12-19-12

Bringing Home The Bacon

If I am to bring home the bacon,
A duty I cannot renege,
I must outrun the fastest,
Or find a slower pig.

The faster pigs taste better,
From tail up to snout,
The slower lazy dullards,
Lethargic, fat, and lout.

The wise man lives the minute,
The lazy man will waste,
The man is molded by pursuit,
Of whichever pig he chased.

J Holt 2-14-12

Watching The Clock

The life that you live will be empty
If you never give all you've got,
You're selling your life by the minute,
If you work watching the clock.

If effort you give can be measured
By how much you make when it stops,
You make of yourself more the pauper,
If you work watching the clock.

If all that you bring to your workplace
Can leave with you when doors are locked,
Then you never really are working,
If you work watching the clock.

If all that you'll do has been settled,
If you bring no heart to the shop,
Your life will be spent like a trifle,
If you spend it watching the clock.

You never will find your real purpose,
You'll never know whether or not,
And you'll never see your true person,
'Til you've given all you've got.

J Holt 4-25-91

A Gentle June Rain
(On A Tin Roofed Barn)

The smell of hay rich in my face,
I deeply breathed it in,
And lost myself in the gentle sounds
Of rain upon the tin,
I yielded all my worries
To the cadence without end,
I felt it wash me as it fell
Outside upon the tin.

All the burdens of my life
Seemed far away just then,
I lost them in the mesmerizing
Sound upon the tin,
I can't explain the mend of rain
God brought to me just then,
As I listened to the music
Of the rain upon the tin.

My thirsty spirit drank the sound
"Til I was full within,
I've stored the memories of that day
I listened near the tin,
I visit with the memories
Of that day like a friend,
I lost myself in gentle sounds
Of rain upon the tin.

J Holt 6-26-91

Spring Shelter

The long limber branches
    Whipped in the breeze,
As the thunderstorm drenched
    The new-leafed trees,
While the robin sat quietly
    Dry as you please,
'Neath the hedge at the
    Corner of the house.

JHolt2-10-83

The Parachutist

There once was a parachutist Bach,
Who landed one day on a rock,
Since the day of that fall
He isn't too tall,
For his kneecaps slid down in his socks.

J Holt 4-5-84

Sunshine for The Children

If the sun shines on the flowers
    And they have it by the hours,
Then for sure they'll blossom
    Pretty as they grow,
But if they've only water
    Without the soil and fodder,
They will live but will no flowers grow.

Children must have love shown,
    Not just a house they call home,
And like the warmest sun
    It must be free,
They need love without condition,
    And freedom of petition,
Sincere enough to meet their deepest needs.

J Holt 3-27-83

Busy

I love the busy life, I do,
I'd rather have it thus,
Rather than to drift along,
Eventually to rust.

I'd rather have too much to do,
Too much, and then some more,
Than to live a life so bland,
That each day is a bore.

J Holt 4-1-85

Worry

Worry will not empty out tomorrow of its sorrow,
Nor apprehension lift the dread of dark,
Fear will multiply and double all your trouble,
Doubt will rob the joy within your heart.

J Holt 3-18-08

Ode To The Stone Caster

A stone caster is one who customizes stones, usually found on corner stones of buildings or at the entrance of estates bearing the family name or coat of arms. After observing my nephew making some large stones, I wrote the following.

There once was a stone caster Walt,
Who made some huge stones for a vault,
He fell in the mold,
And the concrete took hold,
Now I go to the bank to see Walt.

J Holt 9-5-85

Eternal Worth

The only worthwhile way to spend
Your time down here on earth,
Just live your life so what you've done
Will have eternal worth.

J Holt 1-26-90

Why Do We Do It?

We go in debt to dress ourselves
In clothes that say "success,"
And later pay the doctor
To relieve us of our stress.
We hire a tutor to instruct
So that we may impress,
When in truth we crave no life
Of genuine finesse.
We know that we should fill up
'fore the service station's passed,
And kick ourselves for miles and miles,
While walking back for gas.
We frown when others speak to us
Offensively or crass,
And later let our own tongue slip
And decent people gasp.
We get upset when we're in charge
And others show up late,
And later absentmindedly
Forget important dates.
It's part of human nature
That we say and do not do,
They're contradictions in us all,
Except for me and you!

J Holt 2-3-90

Family Reunion Memories

To say 'I remember' is saying I've lived,
Each of your lives part of mine,
Each person's name brings a tug of the heart,
For that's where we all intertwine.

We've planted, each one, our life in the others,
Shared heartaches when living was dark,
And documented years with our laughter,
And stored it all deep in our hearts.

Each one left footprints of life we made living,
And love stains the cloth of our souls,
We have a uniqueness given of God,
A heritage wrapped up in the whole.

J Holt 5-24-06

The Land Of Fantasy

Into the land of fantasy
We all occasionally go,
Where we can dream
And there make it seem,
Our make-believe castles are so.

We daydream of far-away countries,
Where longings are met and relieved,
We stay for awhile
And leave with a smile,
From the land of make believe.

There's much good in wishing and dreaming,
That lifts us from our daily grind,
And we use each day
From lands far away,
The useful things caught in the mind.

Our castles without foundations,
Are places to visit, not stay,
It may not be seeming,
But we build from dreaming,
Our genuine castles each day.

J Holt 1-18-90

Ode to The Fisherman

Stay on the job where you're earning your bread,
And labor as hard as you wish,
Stay as late as the job demands,
But take time out to fish!

Give it your best with the tick of the clock,
Observing the company rules,
Remember all of the training you've had,
And remember which bait to use.

Be faithful to bring home the bacon,
And work every day with your zeal,
Do what you must, but don't let the rust
Collect on your rod and reel!

J Holt 9-20-88

The Lonely Man of Contention

Like dripping unending of water contending
With rocks for its own right of way,
With bitter contention this man, with attrition,
Scolds all that he meets every day,
Scoffing, he thought, whatever was wrought,
Was done without asking his mind,
Bitter words dropping, and dropping, and dropping
On who or whatever he finds.

His days and his nights are filled with his gripes,
Complaining his way through the years,
The rock that is worn with the dropping of scorn
Is the heart that has loved brought to tears,
His insatiable urge to find fault will purge
All kindness and love from his heart,
His endless debate will sow seeds of hate
And cause all who can, to depart.

The rocks are the reason the water sounds lovely
While winding its way to the sea,
The groveling mind of the man of contention
Will never, this simple truth see,
What is accomplished if dropping and dropping
The water will wear the rock through?
The man is rewarded with bitterness hoarded,
What envy has taught him to do.

His mean bitter tone cuts down to the bone
As envy drives on his revenge,
He keeps on believing that he should get even,
As on he goes in his binge,
He never made friends through life to the end,
He chose to live like a churl,
His life of contention, pursing his mission,
Disputing with all of the world.

J Holt 12-10-90

The Daily Fray

The cloth of our soul that we wear every day,
Is often times caught in a difficult way,
And battered and tattered and torn in the fray,
'til seams come unthreaded by end of the day,
   'til we get home.

The unyielding law of necessity drives,
And daily the rat race is hard to survive,
Mid indifferent masses where everyone strives,
But this keeps us going 'til evening is nigh,
   And we go home.

Home is the family and friends you perceive,
Or home is the heart of a friend who believes,
Or kids on the lap and the hugs they receive,
Or just being understood meets a deep need,
   When we get home.

Home, where we find our acceptance complete,
And strength to keep going when we face defeat,
And love, unconditional, supplied in replete,
This mends the daily fray full and compete,
   AH, THIS IS HOME!

J Holt 9-24-90

Procrastination

One of his self-deceptions,
A favorite thing he would say,
He was content in believing,
"I'll do it, but some other day."

Intently he looked on while progress
Went marching right by every day,
There is no successful sincerity,
Intending will bring us no pay.

He sat down beside good intentions,
And traveled no further to be,
He envied success in the others,
While mourning his own poverty.

He honestly thought himself noble,
Vowing to follow it through,
The sweet voice of laziness soothed him,
"Intending is all you must do."

J Holt 1-16-90

The Brutish Man

The brutish man, when young and strong,
Will rule his fellow man with brawn,
He chooses might o'er mind and soul,
In strength he feels secure and whole.

The kind of men who love brute rule,
Make others brutish, also fools,
They've no desire to use the mind,
The brawn is now, the mind takes time.

He who rules with brawn does so,
He will not train his mind to know,
Since muscle gives opinion force
Weak thought is often thus endorsed.

The passing time will take its toll,
On brawny men with shriveled souls,
The brute will need his mind to serve,
When it's just undeveloped nerve.

Carefully choose your path in life
Because you cannot walk it twice,
Treat you mind like it's your friend,
Because you'll have to the end.

The brute who lived life as a knave,
Will often serve as though a slave
In twilight years beyond his brawn
When his own mind can't stand alone.

J Holt 3-4-88

Afterglow of A Hug

A warm contentment lingers
Deep down inside of me,
Which warmly hugs my inmost self,
Making me feel free.

It helps to heal lingering hurt
Long past rejections left,
And quietly mends the one within,
And lets me love myself.

J Holt 11-1-88

Shout Is Clout to The Dumb

Whether or not you raise your voice
Depends on this rule of thumb,
Intelligent people hear when you speak,
But shout is clout to the dumb.

J Holt 3-24-89

Approval

It's hard to explain why we suffer pain
When we feel unapproved of by others,
And normal it seems our best self-esteem
We get from our fathers and mothers.

There's no appetite harder to fight,
Than longings born out of rejection,
And nothing's as strong to fill up the longings,
Like sincere, persistent, affection.

J Holt 8-12-89

Funny Barnyard Scene

The old heifer sneezed, and fell on her knees,
And then fell all the way down,
But he wasn't the kind of man to give up,
He milked her down on the ground.

J Holt 4-22-89

Autonomy

There's a subtle, silent process
That takes place in a child,
That lets him learn self confidence
And think himself worthwhile,
Down inside the core of self
Where personhood abides,
He takes these small defining steps
When he learns to decide.

J Holt 7-29-89

Farewell To The Lazy

The earth would be rid of the lazy,
If they were the only ones here,
With no one to feed them,
None would succeed them,
They never would last out the year.

J Holt 8-7-18

Simple Gifts

I'd rather have the sunshine
Of one sincere, simple gift,
Than all the lovely rainbows,
With their temporary lift,
The sunshine lingers in my heart
And warms me o'er and o'er,
When transitory rainbows
Are not vivid anymore.

J Holt 12-28-89

Beauty

Beauty confined in timed sound
    Is music to our ears,
Beauty confined in people
    Are the children of our years,
Beauty confined in loving trust
    Is friendship to our soul,
Beauty confined in acceptance,
    Matures us, making us whole.

Beauty confined in forgiveness
    Erases hurts and pain,
Beauty confined in courage,
    Lifts us up again,
Beauty in understanding
    Helps us to believe,
Beauty in love opens the heart,
    God's love to receive.

J Holt 8-1-89

Lacing My Shoes

I knew I was loved by my mom and my dad,
Who taught me with don't and the do's,
They always had time for things that were mine,
And had time to lace up my shoes.

Sometimes it was trying to hear past my crying,
When I did things done by young fools,
I still heard applauding and bragging and lauding,
When first I could lace my own shoes.

Soon came the day, I went out to play,
Where others don't play by the rules,
I still found consoling in stored up extolling,
Like when I could lace my own shoes.

So swift goes the time but stored in my mind,
Are mem'ries from which I can chose,
It still does me good, as it once would,
To see Daddy lacing my shoes.

J Holt 8-12-89

The Kids Are Gone, But-----

The miniature shoes on the dresser,
A constant reminding confessor,
That kids passed this way,
And brightened our day,
And grandkids will be their successor.

A mixture of toys in the "camper,"
Evidenced grandparents pamper,
Spoil their grandkids,
Like their parents did,
But not so, their parents to hamper.

Our core life beliefs are not hidden,
But passed on from parents to kids,
Their living is such,
They're so much like us,
And like us, they do what we did.

J Holt 9-18-89

The Make Up of The Day

The words we said were very few,
We had not much to say,
We each could see the other,
'Neath the make-up of the day.

Sometimes we wear our best facade,
When social debts we pay,
I like you best when you're just you,
Not made up for the day.

We pretend at times that we
Are just as others say,
I like the inmost self you are,
Not made up for the day.

One can easily lose himself
In fashion, so they say,
And never know the common life,
Not made up for the day.

We sat in peaceful silence,
Just how long I cannot say,
We found in each sweet solitude,
Not made up for the day.

J Holt 2-25-89

Mining The Heart

There is a heart treasure hidden, unique,
And few understand this treasure to seek,
Common among us, and yet it is rare,
The place where it's hidden, few ever go there.

The inmost person is this hidden treasure,
And only is given in limited measure,
Since few learn the skill of mining the heart,
And so, it is given in very small parts

Man learns of God in hearing His Word,
Responding in faith to show he has heard,
Friends grow more trusting if when they reveal,
Someone is listening and cares how they feel.

Inmost the person first feels his own worth,
When long muted feelings are voiced into birth,
And poured in the hearts of trusting friends,
Somehow, it's a mystery, but there lies the mend.

J Holt 12-25-89

Daddies

Daddies are fathers who've graduated
From the elementary school of "sire,"
To the university of children's hearts,
Where love is the pay for their hire.

Daddies are fathers without a halo,
Without all the trappings of rank,
An ordinary every-day common man,
About his own blemishes, frank.

Daddies are fathers who gladly spend all,
Who strain every sinew providing,
Whose love knows no unit of measure,
Lavished on his own abiding.

Daddies are fathers whose love never turns,
When actions aren't clearly discerned,
Constant, gentle, uninterrupted,
And given when it's not returned.

Daddies are fathers whom children can touch,
Whose lap is a haven with hugs,
A shoulder to cry on when woes are too much,
And heartstrings so easily tugged.

Daddies are fathers who help you find answers,
To know what life is about,
A warm-hearted welcome, for he always leaves,
The latchstring of love hanging out.

Daddies are fathers with deep satisfaction,
If this rule is practiced and learned,
Love with your heart, and love without measure
Is just what you get in return.

J Holt 12-26-89

The Optimist

The optimist sees the acorn,
And sees the mighty oak,
The pessimist sees the nut and thinks
The tree is but a joke.

The pessimist seeing faults and failures,
Thinks that's all you'll be,
The optimist sees persistence,
Like acorns growing trees.

J Holt 11-26-89

The End Is the Beginning

Sometimes when you think you are finished with
life and your dreams have all come to an end,
And inside you feel you are ceasing to care as you
did when you once did begin,
When you feel you're empty of stuff that it takes
to continue to do and to dare,
When you start to think your dreams have all
vanished as quickly as steam in the air.

When you start to question your calling in life that
you felt so secure in before,
When most of the people that you thought were
faithful you feel you can't trust them no more,
Sometimes when your hoarded resources are gone
and you tremble with fear in your heart,
You think it's all ended because you depended on
all of those things at the start.

What looks like an ending is just a beginning,
remember that you're in God's hands,
He won't let you drown when it seems you are
down so deep that you won't rise again,
God is the master at taking the pieces of lives
That are left in a mess,
And giving them purpose, direction, and meaning
when He starts the small things to bless.

What looks like an ending is just a beginning
Remember that God is not man,
All your confusion will have its conclusion
When you see the light of God's plan,
When you think it's over, it's finished, and you
think you won't see the sun rise again,
The place where you gave up and thought you
were done for is just where the Lord will begin!

J Holt 1-26-86

Ode to The Cook

Here lie the bones of Hilda the cook,
Her recipe she forgot when she cooked,
She tasted her stew
To see if t'was true,
But her life with her stew she took.

J Holt 2-11-86

Bad Apples

The vintage saying is that "One
Bad apples Spoils the lot,"
Its influence cannot be contained,
Its stimulus is rot.

Bad will always drive out good,
No matter what you do,
This law is irrevocable,
Like one and one make two.

Counterfeit will not improve
Though mixed with genuine,
Though hid behind a bright façade,
It spoils the good in time.

Good and bad can't co-exist,
And each remain the same,
Bad will hold its quality,
But good just good in name.

Always choose with utmost care
The ones you and love and cherish,
In intimate talks and prolonged walks
With them, you live or perish.

J Holt 7-21-87

Letting Go

One of the hardest things parents must do,
Let children follow the path that they choose,
Show them, sincerely, you really do care,
And unconditionally, your love will be there.

We learn the wise choices with practice, and so,
With trial and with error the good ones we know,
Each course that is taken is proven with time,
As are the mistakes of the choosing a crime.

The thing that rejoices the parents the most,
One of which wise parents surely will boast,
Because when their children have learned to think,
Though their boat takes on water, it never will sink!

J Holt 12-31-89

Old Parents

So often the role of the parent and child
Is reversed in the twilight of years,
When strong arms grow feeble,
And sharp minds grow misty,
And courage is smothered with fears.

J Holt 1-10-86

Small Men

Small is the man who thinks he is rich,
By the cut of his clothes,
Or the weave or the stitch.

J Holt 1-16-86

Hug Me!

The things in life that really bug us,
Bug us less when someone hugs us!

J Holt 10-15-86

Loyalty

Generally, the man who rows the boat,
And does his best to keep it afloat,
Loves the boat too much to knock it,
And rows the boat rather than rock it.

J Holt 2-18-87

Situational Ethics

A man's a fool to change the rules,
That he may win the game,
And small indeed if all his needs,
Are met with meager fame.

J Holt 4-28-87

As A Man Thinketh

What you think is what you are,
Your thoughts will cast the mold,
The mind will shape your character,
Your body, and your soul.

Circumstance may seem to be
Beyond your own control,
But things will happen as you wish
Them to down in your soul.

You never rise above the life
You live within your mind,
Nor pass the mental boundaries
Your thought life has defined.

You will never walk a path
Where you feel all alone,
If in your mind you've traveled there,
Then you feel right at home.

If you want to build your life,
Then you must understand,
It is wrought with tools of thought
And then built with your hand.

A single passing thought can seem
Without influence, and small,
But we reap the thing it brought,
When it we can't recall.

This is a simple, powerful truth,
Which makes us all distinct,
We always reap just what we sow,
We are just what we think.

J Holt 2-19-87

Reaching Higher

Just for today I'll try to do more,
Try to go farther than I've gone before,
Rise above average in some small way,
Better for God just for today.

J Holt 12-1-86

Springtime in Texas

Flowers bloomed by the old board fence
Urged on by the morning sun,
Birds fluttered in the hedge near the house,
The nesting season has begun,

The mockingbird perched on the mailbox
Where the postman stops each day,
His full-throated song in the early dawn
Signals the season's fray.

Haley's comet circled the sky
The visit according to plan,
The grass, the flowers, and longer hours,
Spring has come again

J Holt 2-15-86

Time Passes So Fast

One hundred sixty-eight hours are numbered
In measure of time called a week,
Passing in seconds and minutes and hours,
Permanently and so fleet!

J Holt 7-21-87

The Fat Man

There once was a fat man from Perth,
Who thought his girth was he worth,
He sacrificed health,
For what he thought wealth,
And shortened his life on the earth.

J Holt 4-28-87

How To Succeed

You need not be a genius,
Or flim-flam man with flair,
Whatever spot you hold in life,
Just always be all there.

J Holt 11-24-87

Look Beyond the Trees

Someone has said that you can't see the forest,
While looking too close at the trees,
That we miss the grandeur and power and beauty,
If branches are all that we see.

Hilltops and mountains and valleys and prairies,
Become something special with trees,
But we miss the mend of the glen if we only
See branches that sway in the breeze.

The language of solace to nourish the spirit,
The forest so quietly breathes,
But wearisome prattle is only the rattle
Of branches resisting the breeze.

Deep in the forest are undisturbed places,
Like far away islands at sea,
But there's no enamor to come from the clamor
'Neath branches that sway in the breeze.

A view of the forest bespeaks a completeness
That says a man's spirit is free,
But small the person whose vision is filled up
With just a few boughs that he sees.

May God give us vision to see all the forest,
To dream and be all we can be,
And not be contented with pleasantly scented
Branches that sway in the breeze.

When you see no reason of hope for the future,
When you feel there's nothing for thee,
It could be the view that you need of the forest,
Is simply obscured by the trees.

J Holt 3-2-87

The Purpose Of A Poem

The purpose of a poem is to
    Help us find a way,
To find the right expression,
    For the things we cannot say,
We wrestle with our feelings
    If we shut them up inside,
But often times a simple rhyme
    Will help us to confide.

J Holt 3-14-83

Sunshine For The Heart

If the sun shines on the flowers,
And they have it by the hours,
Then for sure they'll blossom
Pretty as they grow,
But if they've only water
And plenty root and fodder,
Though alive, they'll
Seldom petals grow.

Children must have love shown,
Not just a place in your home,
And like the warmest sun
It must be free,
Love without condition,
And freedom of petition,
Sincere enough to
Meet their deepest needs.

J Holt 3-22-83

The Heart Song

Buried deep in the heart of my heart
Is an endless and beautiful song,
I've never heard its tune or its words,
But I've felt it overpoweringly strong.

I cannot name the composer,
Nor tell you the meter or key,
Nor tell you the source of the music,
But I know it masters me.

No genius of meter or measure,
Could set it to orchestra strings,
No master of words of the language,
Could write this heavenly thing.

God holds the secret for keeping,
We savor a taste now and then,
He is the source of the music,
Sung in the souls of men.

J Holt 9-26-97

Growing Up

I can do it myself Dad,
    I'm getting bigger you know,
Again and again I hear it,
    Baby is starting to grow,
I can do it myself Dad,
    I can tie shoes myself,
Don't put your hands on the handle,
    I can ride myself.

I can do it myself dad,
    Buttons and zippers I know,
I'm no longer a baby,
    I'm big now, doesn't it show?
You must let me do it myself dad,
    By doing I learn that I can,
And when I see your approval,
    The courage will make me a man.

J Holt 4-8-83

A Hug Would Make My Day

Something marvelously wonderful happens,
Down in the heart of a child,
When given an unsolicited hug,
You're telling him (her) "You're worthwhile."

J Holt 4-7-83

The Land Of Lying

Life in the land of lying,
Is a comfortable place to be,
It adds false spice to simple life
And makes one think he's free.

Pretense is a hiding place,
Harmless, yet deceptive,
As children play throughout the day,
And never be decisive.

The mind that feeds on fantasy
Can't comprehend the truth,
Small is the mind of the liar,
When make-believe can soothe.

J Holt 3-17-08

Success

Give me the man who'll do the job,
Day after day after day,
Give me the man who'll tackle the task,
And always earn his pay.

Give me the man who faithfully
Always fills his place,
Give me the man, who, on his on
Works at a quickened pace.

Give me the man who won't complain,
And negative words won't say,
Give me the man who won't give up,
Or quit in the heat of the day.

Success will not come to the quitter,
But to the one who will try,
Who won't give up, no matter the task,
Success will not be denied.

J Holt 10-5-83

A Candle

A candle keeps you company
When you feel all alone,
It warms the room dispelling gloom,
And makes it more like home,
It's not bombastic friendships
That see you through the night,
It's the silent, flickering flame
In darkness giving light.

J Holt 12-13-92

Ode to The Omelet Maker

There is a good omelet maker Jim,
Nobody makes omelets like him,
He made them so great,
That I overate,
And now I am no longer slim.

J Holt 11-17-18

The Fool and The Fireplace

A shivering man came close to the hearth
And stirred up the coals on the grate,
Fleeting the moment of flames in the coals,
Then dying to ashes of fate.

Bitter the tone of his voice as he spoke,
The cold was numbing his feet,
"Why is it I must give you some wood
Before you will give me some heat?"

J Holt 4-29-96

The Toothpick

The toothpick is a curious stick,
With sharp points on each end,
And when you cannot brush your teeth,
The toothpick is your friend.

J Holt 10-10-09

The Butterfly

If you want a close look
    At the butterfly,
You must look very quickly
    As it flutters by.

J Holt 10-20-09

I Wear A Smile

I wear the same smile everyday
    And wear it all day long,
It's not because I have no ills
    And not because I'm strong.

I do not smile because my friends
    Have proven themselves true,
Nor do I smile because I'm paid
    For everything I do.

I do not smile because I'm free
    From every ache and pain,
And I don't smile because my loss
    Is smaller than my gain.

I do not smile because I have
    The money that I need,
Nor smile because each thing I do
    Won't fail but will succeed.

I smile because I know God's laws
    That govern will not change,
And every man's success or failures
    Are not prearranged.

I smile because God hears the prayers
   Of such a simple man,
I smile because God gives me light
   To see and understand.

God gives me opportunities,
   I see with trusting faith,
He lets me choose my wages,
   And thereby choose my fate.

J Holt 2-10-98

In A Tizzy

When we're busy in a tizzy,
Dreams will come in endless number,
Some disturbing, some perturbing,
Some enhancing sweetest slumber.

Dreams we mold when we are bold,
Are dreams that give us purpose,
Dreams we lose because we choose,
Are nightmares, living with us.

J Holt 10-12-09

The Mongrel Millionaire

I want to introduce you to
   The mongrel millionaire,
He seems so unbecoming in
   The finery he wears,
And out of place when mingling
   With the other millionaires,
Displaying all the symbols of his
   Wealth with vulgar flair.

He has a million dollars but
   He's not a millionaire,
Nor wealthy though he has perfected
   Putting on the air,
Though covered with learned etiquette
   His boorishness is there,
Wealth promotes the odious but
   Leaves him unaware.

J Holt 3-31-97

Wretched

Wretched committed a horrible crime,
Without doubt worthy of death,
He spoke of his own execution
With excitement in every breath.

He seemed not to think of his loved ones,
Who would miss him after a while,
He dismissed all of his carnage,
And said with an innocent smile.

"I'm wearing the robes of the sovereign,
Worn out, discarded, and old,
I'm riding out to the gallows,
In a chariot gilded with gold."

J Holt 1-24-11

Disadvantage is Advantage

The night must come with cloak of dark,
And we must see it through,
If we would reap the wealth of dawn,
And taste the morning dew.

The chill and gloom of darkness is
Unpleasant to the soul,
But in the night, we gain the sight
Above the status-quo.

What looks like disadvantage is
Advantage when you're done,
As night-formed dew drops glistering
In the morning sun.

J Holt 9-9-93

Don't Sweat The Small Stuff

The folks who sweat the small stuff,
Perspire the day away,
There's no such thing as small stuff,
To folks who live that way.

J Holt 12-20-96

Again!

Keep your spirit up and you will win!
Treat not trite the power of a grin,
Persistence has more muscle in the end,
And exhilaration bursts from "try again"!

You cannot tame the power or the thrill
Of knowing that your winning is the will,
So, count no opportunity as nil,
And keep on keeping on until and until!!!

J Holt 11-4-93

If You Faint in The Day of Adversity
  (Proverbs 24:10)

If trees find their ample water supply
Too near the top of the ground,
The roots that hold the tree upright,
Never go very far down.

Trees with shallow roots easily can stand,
And look as good as the rest.
Until the times of storms and droughts
Bring nature's cruelest tests.

Most people flourish in serving the Lord,
As long as it's easy and fun.
Then comes the trials we all suffer,
And see who remains when they're gone.

The trails are not meant to defeat us,
Our roots grow much deeper in tests,
For God knows when our faith grows deeper,
We're stronger and serve Him the best.

J Holt 2-15-92

The Bond of The Heart

I've heard it said by sages
That the spirit never ages,
That the heart of man remains forever young,
Like good music in good measure
With the passing years more treasured,
We love it more each time we hear it sung.

There is a bond 'tween spirits
And the thing that so endears it,
A simple mystery people seldom see,
Not found in some behavior
As though conduct were our savior,
Nor is it found in some philosophy.

How strange a thing to some it seems,
That love can flow in endless streams,
That hearts can love and never know a drought,
The spirit wills to one the heart,
When it's accepted, bonding starts,
And that's what love and friendship are about.

J Holt 6-19-92

Rowing Against the Tide

The timid man waits on the shore ever dreaming
Of faraway places where others abide,
He lives in his dreams, he never will row,
Against ever changing tides.

Enchanting tales fill him with dreams,
Of sailing through gales on the main,
He longed for the wine they earned in living,
To row was too much of a strain.

He saw the horizon far out at sea,
He dreamed alone until he died,
He never took risks one takes in living,
He saw not the world, just the tide.

J Holt 10-8-93

The Life House

There are no houses ever built
Less needing vindication,
Than those which rest on purpose,
Defying explanation.

The heart-house has a beauty,
Alone in its perfection,
And glows with pristine purity,
Whose strength is its protection.

Few will build a life-house,
Though blueprints are supplied,
But those sincere in seeking,
Will never be denied.

J Holt 11-24-93

False Guilt

I suppose there's nothing else
More blinds an honest man,
Than feeling guilty, when the guilt
He cannot understand.

J Holt 2-17-92

Good Medicine

A hug gives something to one receiving it,
And something for one who gives,
And something stirs in the heart of each,
And wakes up, beginning to live.

That long dormant, unexplained something,
Silently, was ignored,
Was stirred in a way I cannot say,
As it never was stirred before.

You hugged several times 'fore I felt it,
I loved the new feeling, though strange,
It was a long while since my heart smiled,
Inside I was rearranged.

Exhilarating joy raced through my mind,
I couldn't explain it or say,
Thirsty, I soaked up the gentle rain,
And drank it again all day.

J Holt 4-23-91

Deadly Faults

There is a deadly thing we do,
A fault that does us in,
It's forming habits that destroy,
And treat them like a friend.

We seldom feel the tightening grip,
Of things to our demise,
And seldom see the simple steps,
To bring them down to size.

J Holt 11-20-92

Secluded Island

I've found a quiet secluded isle,
Where oft' I go and rest awhile,
I walk beneath the ferns and trees,
And fill my lungs with ocean breeze,
Its wavelets die upon the shore
With slightest murmur, and what's more,
No government has owned this place,
And it's not claimed by any race.

It's off the beaten path for ships,
And off the list for tourist trips,
I find such meaningful repose,
In this place where no one goes,
This restoring place is free,
But most are blind and cannot see,
This place of rest for weary men,
If found in hearts of dearest friends.

J Holt 11-9-85

John Holt   Poems That Matter – Book One

Death of A Snowflake

It seemed to be a tragic death,
Yet no one was surprised,
The poison, just a common one,
As all who knew, surmised.

He walked along, haphazard,
As though he was exempt,
He regarded no one,
A devilish, simple, imp.

His ego, a most fragile thing,
Would often start to sink,
In simple situations,
When he was forced to think.

The poison was invisible,
Yet plain for all to see,
That fateful day, the day he drank
Responsibility.

J Holt 12-27-18

Old Mose

A far-sighted snake named old Mose,
Once held his sweet girlfriend up close,
He said with a grin,
"You have such smooth skin,"
She said, "I'm an old garden hose."

J Holt 12-14-05

Irritation

I have an itch I cannot reach
And therefore, cannot scratch,
The irritation, though unseen,
An ever-present fact.

Carefully tend your garden,
One weed will remain,
Though vast and full your learning,
One quest will tease the brain.

Though you acquire all wealth of earth,
One penny more is gain,
Though very careful with your health,
Still there's one more pain.

The finest dog can have one flea,
The finest art one blot,
The craving one will never be
Content with what he's got.

The best of life will always have
One nagging thread of strife,
Do you do the small things,
Or larger things in life?

J Holt 10-7-15

The Mantle of The Day

The first thoughts of the day
Are the ones that tend to stay,
Deciding everything we say or do,
If haphazard or well planned,
If or not we understand,
This mantle makes us false or makes us true.

The first thoughts we define
Become the mantle of the mind,
As though an unseen force drew us along,
It makes the strong feel weak,
Gives courage to the meek,
 And fills the place the mind feels best at home.

God made man the master
Of where his mind may pasture,
And thus, become a beast or moral man,
The acid test of character
Will show in what you're after,
And whether or not you chose to understand.

J Holt 1-7-99

Talk Is Cheap

The man who talks of noble things
And never does the deeds,
Is like a garden, well planned out,
But growing only weeds.

A man is self-deceived who thinks
Plans along succeed,
Flowers you must cultivate,
Neglect will grow the weeds.

Great intentions slake the thirst
Of slothful, thoughtless, fools,
Who glibly estimate their words,
Can circumvent the rules.

J Holt 2-28-01

A Philosophical View of Things

Few are the men craving honest refinement,
And seek it with all of their souls,
And settle in comfortably into that life,
And need not the dirt of cajole.

Civilization is never sustained,
By men with their brains in their belly,
Who worship the gods of taste and pleasure,
And celebrate dilly and dally.

Woe to the man who won't rise above doing
Things that are natural, with ease,
Who rather finds starving less painful than thinking
And won't understand what he sees.

The world is a difficult place at the best,
No man is exempt from the strife,
And every man living down here on the planet
Has chances to better his life.

Whenever the sun sets on your span of living,
And day turns to night in the west,
God will then judge of your faith and your doing,
Will He measure you a success?

J Holt 3-8-96

You Never Will Know

You never will know what you're made of
As long as you lean on another,
Your thoughts and your best aspirations
Will never take shape in your brother.

Thoughts are the smallest slight urgings of will,
But die if not nurtured with might,
Action gives might to creation in man,
When day shines on dreams of the night.

J Holt l6-23-97

The Athlete Lee

There once was an athlete Lee,
Who wanted big biceps, you see,
He swallowed his steroids,
Coughed them up into his adenoids,
Now his nose is big as a tree.

J Holt 12-23-05

The All-American Pig

He has a pot belly that wobbles like jelly,
And can't be contained by his belt,
He has no perspective, nor is he reflective,
His mind only measures what's felt.

So loudly he curses the men with full purses,
And swears that each one is a crook,
He hates the I Q of the one who can do
Successful things writ in the book.

He works at his job with a mindset to rob,
And pouts if denied any pleasure,
He goes on demanding with no understanding,
The indolent gather no treasure.

He thinks he is thriving, when he's just surviving,
When he has a mouth full of munch,
He's fooling himself with what he has left,
He's selling his soul for his lunch.

J Holt 2-9-94

The Anvil

The anvil will outlast the hammer,
For nothing it yields to the blows,
While hammers are pounding the metal,
The anvil is steady below.

Repeating the pounding which forces the metal,
The hammer will give of itself,
The anvil remains unaffected, the hammer
Wears out in the heat of the heft.

The unnoticed core of the anvil
Endures, no matter the fray,
The prestigious hammers of fashion,
Will pass, in limited days.

J Holt 10-29-95

Robin Hood

I waited for this Robin Hood
To give me my just due,
To rob the rich and give it all
To folks like me and you.

I waited just like Cinderella,
For the magic wand,
I waited, desperately hoping,
While time kept marching on.

I learned the truth about this "Hood,"
I saw through "Cinderella,"
I don't trust thieves and magic wands,
To put food on my table.

God supplies my daily needs,
But this, I understand,
These fables are just fables,
You earn it with your hands.

J Holt 1-4-97

My Guinea Pig Ted

Here lies the bones of my guinea pig Ted,
He endlessly pushed on the cage with his head,
One night he slipped through,
There was naught I could do,
And that was the end of poor Ted.

J Holt 12-9-05

The Security of The Familiar

The thing that stops the average man,
That keeps him from success,
That drenches any burning flame,
Hope kindles in his breast,
Is something overpowering,
Elusive to define,
Is the awesome magnetism
Of familiar things of mind.

J Holt 6-2-97

Thinker

Thinker longed to find secrets
Of men known for deeper thought,
Immersing himself, he struggled,
But surfaced still untaught,
He loved many ancient deceptions,
Which people long had believed,
He found many laws unbreakable,
Leaving him unrelieved.

J Holt 6-9-09

Urgency of Goals

There is a fire that burns inside a man,
When dreams ignite ambition with good sense,
And urgency of goals concocts a plan,
Generating faith that won't relent.

Perpetually, aggressively, consuming,
Exploding in time to bring success,
Vaporizing status quo's assuming,
With common touch of genuine finesse.

J Holt 10-8-98

Pearls Before Swine

Cast not your pearls before the swine,
They've no taste for things divine,
They measure life by a different line,
    They're Hogs!

J Holt 11-30-92

To lighten up the Load

He gave deep thought to what he brought,
And this was his conclusion,
"Is the place to which I go
Real or just illusion?"

J Holt 10-5-11

As the Child Is Bent

They shape and mold the spirit,
And to certain things endear it,
Who raise the child and mold it with their talk.
And everything imprinted
On the child is surely vented,
In the way of life, the child will walk.

The child will live and manage
With the blessing and the damage,
And duplicate the parents in the same,
And every generation
Is a human life reflection,
Exactly passing on the family name.

Fate will make exception
For those, who by election,
Plant and grow a different set of mind.
The law of first imprinting,
Will here, in time, be venting,
And in the child, clearly be defined.

J Holt 11-18-97

Essie and Effie

Essie and Effie were sisters,
I knew them both very well,
Essie brought something fresh to each day,
Effie brought miserable tales.

Essie could warm hearts by smiling,
Her sweetness glowed like a crown,
Effie's face broadcast her misery,
Twisted by permanent frown.

Family would oft visit Essie,
Feasting on her sweeter heart,
Effie served up her worst gloom and woe,
Drowning the sunshine with dark.

Essie and Effie are gone now,
In memory Essie will stay,
Effie is buried somewhere obscure,
No one remembers the place.

J Holt 4-30-98

If You Will Try

You could have a purpose consuming,
Too perfect to ever deny,
But if you refuse the effort,
Your powerful purpose will die.

You could have the greatest of blueprints,
The finest that money can buy,
But genius in planning is worthless,
If you never start out to try.

You may have the greatest of friendships,
Those who will always stand by,
Friends cannot make you successful,
As long as you never do try.

Many are stunned when they find out,
Success is not dreamed or a lie,
Anyone really can do it,
If only they get in and try.

Mountains aren't moved by some magic,
And riches not earned by some sly,
A drink from the well of success can be yours,
If only you'll get in and try.

J Holt 5-1-98

The Pioneer Man

An understanding pioneer man
Journeyed to the west,
He did not take his precious things,
Just what he thought was best.

The trail was long, the horses strong,
And so, the tale is told,
'til hills and rivers made demands
To lighten up the load.

He gave deep thought to what he brought,
And this was his conclusion,
"Is the place to where I go,
Real or just illusion?"

J Holt 10-5-11

Heartaches

God will give enough heartaches
To keep you humble in life,
If He did not give the heartaches,
He could not add the spice.

J Holt 11-23-96

The Diamond

A gentle jeweler happened on a
    Market place one day,
Thoughtfully he looked among
    Some trinkets on display,
The sunlight on a hand-worn stone
    Gave back a deep rich hue,
"Ah" said he beneath his breath,
    "There's value down in you."

He gathered up some lesser things
    And bought them with the stone,
He pocketed his secret prize and
    Hurried to his home,
He doffed his coat and boots and
    Poured himself some steaming brew,
He brought out the hand-worn stone and
    And said, "I must know you."

He listened close to hear the silence
    Of the roughened stone,
"Oh, I've been bought and sold again,
    Will this be my new home?"
"This is your home," the jeweler said,
    "And this is it for keeps,
I must know what's down inside the
    Sunlit hue that sleeps."

A crackling fire, some steaming brew,
    The jeweler and the rock,
"What's beneath this hardened rough
    You're wearing for a frock,
How is it no one else has noticed
    What I saw today?
Your time-worn edges tell of many
    Hands along the way."

"I've been passed around and bought
    And sold by common man,
They liked the bit of hue they saw
    But did not understand,
Diamonds have endurance and
    They like that quality,
They had not skill to get beyond
    The rough that covers me.

It takes care of heart and mind and
    Purpose in the touch,
And greatest skill to do no harm
    When you remove the rough,
I'm not afraid for you to see
    Behind this coarse façade,
I've diamond sparkle to the heart,
    A gift to me from God."

The jeweler set his chisel in the crack
    Whence came the hue,
The hardened shell crumbled and
    The shattered pieces flew,
The crackling fire reflected in
    The room around the man,
He could not speak, but stared
    Into the diamond in his hand.

J Holt 10-4-96

Faith and Intellect

Faith and intellect will fight
    If both participate,
Faith believes impossible,
    Intellect debates,
Intellect will scorn at trust,
    And crown faith as a dunce,
Faith sees the hand of Providence,
    And faith will serve you lunch.

J Holt 3-8-99

Ode to Ego

He was too wonderful for words,
So full and rich his charm,
He held such sway o'er common folks,
It almost caused alarm.

His counsel was so deep, he said,
They lived by what he spoke,
They clamored for his friendship
And laughed at all his jokes.

His leadership was awesome,
His people skills adored,
It is a shame that Ego
Is not with us anymore.

No one really knew him
As he thought himself to be,
He fed on self with nothing left
To face reality.

His body's in the casket,
Cold and void of breath,
Cause he looked into the mirror,
And hugged himself to death.

   J Holt 6-7-91

The Shortest Way Home

Experience travels with Providence,
Its hand in Life is shown,
Patiently showing the longest way 'round,
Is often the shortest way home.

No one lives without effort,
Obtaining for free is not known,
Fools never learn the longest way 'round,
Is really the shortest way home.

The ignorant trifle to thwart the Immutable,
Thinking Him mere flesh and bone,
Wise men will see that the longest way 'round,
Is always the shortest way home.

The wise man will listen and labor the mystery,
Seeking God in His Word known,
And Providence, planning the longest way 'round,
Is surest to get you to home.

The fool in refraction will seek for the simple,
But Patience will not be disowned,
Kept by the world for amusement, the fool,
Is orphaned when he thinks he's home.

Experience will never take short cuts in life,
Refusing all pretense as known,
Rewards are the richest the longest way 'round,
And surely, the shortest way home.

J Holt 1-7-02

Never Give Gifts

Never give gifts without reason,
It speaks of a slavish fear,
Never beg for affection,
Nor bribe those whom fate has brought near.

Never doubt God in your thinking,
He already knows of the day,
Submit to your place in His calling,
And thus, He will see to your pay.

Only help those who are helpless,
Not those pretending their plight,
Rescue no fool unrepentant,
His foolishness you underwrite.

Never descend to the scorners,
To do so, you make yourself small,
They have mastered the negative,
They force you to drink of their gall.

Never resist failure's lessons,
For therein you find your success,
Gain through your personal trials,
Wisdom that brings excellence.

J Holt 9-13-07

The Uncommon Common Man

The greatest of all men among us
Are not those who think and invent,
It's not the deep mind of the gifted,
Nor those with plenty to spend,
Stand up and applaud if you will please,
The one, without natural bend,
Who rises, to walk with the mighty,
Against his own meager imprint.

J Holt 12-1-97

God Set A Time

God set a season when
    The trees and flowers grow,
He set a time for summer,
    And set a time for snow,
He set a nesting season for the
    Calling whippoorwill,
He set a time for you and me
    According to His will.

J Holt 6-10-88

The Obviation of Buford Jones

I ain't skeered that Ah mite fell,
Cuz problums cume that I can't tell,
Dummer men have dune good, so kin I,
Men who make it ain't so smart,
The just got it in thair hart,
And they ain't frayed to tak a chance and try.

I ain't edgycated but,
I jus won't live down in a rut,
Obsequiousness binds like ah chain,
I have knowed that I kin learn,
And risk ain't fatal, I discerned,
Persistence stokes the fire inside my brain.

J Holt 11-3-98

Rejection

That which totally devastates
A person's self-esteem,
Is that which says-
   "You're not worthwhile",
Or makes it so to seem.

J Holt 3-8-83

One Small Rose

A small rose bloomed by the backyard fence,
Though no one saw it there,
Just like the rose on the palace lawn,
Its fragrance filled the air.

J Holt 11-3-85

Ode to The Poet Carpenter

Hay-Cuh-Luh-Cay-Cuh, the smiling man said,
And he quoted some rhyme as he passed,
He seemed to be genuinely happy, and yet,
The sad look in his eye held me fast.

Verse after verse of good rhyme he could say,
With inflection of voice he intoned,
He quoted the famous and those yet obscure,
With passion that made each one live on.

He sang a short song with voice deep and strong,
And compassion that tugged at my heart,
It seemed he restrained his desire to sing on,
As he picked up his tools to depart.

How is it such talent remains unrefined,
And multiplied blessings are lost,
What restrains such a creative heart,
Why should it all be for naught?

J Holt 9-20-85

The Pendulum Swings Where It's Been

I've heard people say that it never is wise
To be harsh in tone when you speak,
For sooner or later those hard, spoken words,
Are just the ones you will meet.

Don't spend all the cash in your pocket,
For some kind of cheap, useless ditty,
For should the time come when necessity calls,
You're stuck with that same needless pretty.

Don't follow the urge that tells you to spend,
In irresistible sales,
The money you "save" will further enslave,
And lead you to financial jail.

Don't be too calloused when dealing with people,
When they cannot help you succeed,
Sooner or later the nameless and faceless,
Will be just the ones you will need.

Don't wait 'til tomorrow to give all your roses,
Or send love to those you hold dear,
Don't put off "I love you" or limit your hugging,
The memories will keep you both near.

John Holt   Poems That Matter – Book One

Never use pressure to bend someone's thinking,
To see things the way that you do,
Sooner or later when they are enlightened,
They'll probably turn and hate you.

Don't be too hard when you are in charge,
And someone beneath you is wrong,
In sowing and reaping we each have our turn,
Of failing with someone who's strong.

People aren't mindless or their lives design-less,
If they don't do things that impress,
It's always surprising to see people rising,
While others live on in distress.

If we've dealt in kindness with those left behind us,
And we travel back once again,
The trip is a trial and never a failure,
When viewed through the eyes of a friend.

The Pendulum travels its pathway relentless
Returning to where it began
Revealing the truth of your personal living
And dealings with every man

J Holt 1-7-90

An Organized Mind

An organized mind is a very good sign,
That people are working with hustle,
Working with brain is much less strain,
Than doing your work with muscle.

We must understand that time not planned,
Can slip through your fingers so fast,
Schedule your work and you'll never hurt,
For time you've spent that is past.

You won't have to run to get it all done,
If you thought it through yesterday,
With meaningful rest you will do your best,
And still have some time for play.

J Holt 1-22-90

Home

When day is dark, I rest my heart,
My home, my simple dwelling,
Accumulated inventory,
Is hardly worth the telling,
I've a place to warm my face
And leave my troubles awhile,
My spirit is nourished to better flourish,
And face the day with a smile.

J Holt 11-20-93

The Wordsmith

I'm a simple wordsmith,
Painting pictures with my rhyme,
Subtly seeing people,
And visiting their time.

Coaxing timid thoughts to speak
Of their own time and place,
Using them to carefully paint,
The life into the face.

J Holt 12-17-17

An Inch of Time

"I would give my millions
    To buy an inch of time,"
Cried the mighty English queen,
    Knowing she was dying.

You cannot buy one heartbeat
    When it's your time to die,
You can't expand your life one breath,
    No matter how you try.

Mankind strains his brain and purse,
    Before his life is gone,
The force of time keeps passing as
    Life's clock keeps ticking on.

The Unseen God set each man's clock,
    Before he was conceived,
Could see, or know, or understand,
    Believe or disbelieve.

J Holt 3-20-11

Time II

Yesterday will not return,
We only have today,
Tomorrow is beyond our grasp,
In God's eternal day.

Time dictates our daily lives,
It stands alone in power,
The wiser man will never waste,
The value of an hour.

Yesterday will fade with time
Tis futile so to yearn,
Time took it with it when it passed,
Never to return.

J Holt 1-30-19

Water Seeks Its Level

Water seeks its level,
   No matter what the tilt,
It rushes on to meet itself,
   From where it first was spilt.
Quality meets principle
   No matter where they're built,
High in moral standard,
   Or below the moral silt.

J Holt 7-23-93

Habits

Habits which we form in youth,
Be they wholesome or uncouth,
Cost us nail or cost us tooth,
Will give us peace or fears.

Some are friends enhancing life,
Some are parasites of strife,
Some add gall and some add spice,
As each one flavors years.

Some are friends and some are foe,
In foolish youth we do not know
In time which way our life will go,
To joy or to tears.

In brazen confidence we choose,
Wisdom speaks but we refuse,
Some will bless and some abuse,
Some bring comfort, some bring tears.

If these won't change, where shall we find
Contented life with peace of mine?
Give good habits your best time,
And strengthen them with years.

J Holt 12-22-17

The Unknown Trail

Life is like an unknown trail,
With unknown things ahead,
Some men find excitement,
Some men go with dread.

Those who do not walk the trail
Because they cannot go,
Feast on life's fulfillment,
Because they want to know.

Those who do not walk the trail,
Because they will not go,
Grovel for their life because
The refuse to know.

J Holt 1-13-18

Significance

He leaned on the hoe and looked on the row,
And wondered why he was so poor,
Why no one sought out his wisdom,
Why none beat a path to his door.

The devil devised to work his demise,
And soon had the perfect plan,
A scheme designed for destruction,
To bring down this simple man.

He said, "It is plain you have a good brain,
But out here no one will know,
I have a cause that will use you,
Where all of your wisdom will show."

Hear his sad wail, pathetically pale,
"I thought I was making a difference,"
He gave the vast wealth of personal self,
For a minuscule significance.

He suffered no harm on his lowly farm,
He longed his sin to erase,
He battered his soul for glittering gold,
And lost the jewel of his place.

J Holt 10-15-09

Materialism

"If we could get enough of the satisfying stuff,
Contentment would be captive in our hands,"
Life they are professing, but empty in possessing,
Gnawing thirst is all they comprehend.

Imaginary need is the seed of growing greed,
Driving man to crave more and more,
Never can they stop to savor what they've got,
Elusive is the gain they're living for.

Material corsages like distant heat mirages,
"Only he is happy who is king,"
They do not understand that they do not understand,
There's nothing for the soul in a thing.

Onward grind the mills of the human-mind spiels,
And never in this life do they desist,
The temporary bread speaks when they are dead,
"The things you sold me for do not exist."

J Holt 10-1-13

This Newfangled Electronic Age

I was in my car one day
Trying to find Main Street way,
The situation was not going well,
I plugged my Garmin Nuvi
In the thing that plays my movies,
The lights began to blink, and my horn wailed.

A light came on said "Oil is low,"
I knew for sure that was not so,
I drove on to find my destination,
Very shortly things got worse,
The display said, "You're in reverse,"
It filled my mind with dreadful consternation.

I glanced back at my display
For what instructions it might say,
I was wondering just what I should do,
The light came on "Your battery is dead,"
And then the strangest thing it said,
"Brush your teeth as soon as you are through."

It said, "Be sure and check your mail,"
It looks like thunderstorms and hail,
Bring home a loaf of bread, a dozen eggs,"
It said, "Back up and then turn left,"
It said, "You'll never cut yourself
With this razor when you shave your legs."

It said, "Turn left just at the curve,
And if your kids get on your nerves,
Satisfaction or a full refund,"
It said, "Be sure to go and vote,
And if you have a scratchy throat,
Motor oil will help to clear your lungs."

I've been told this modern age,
Computers are the present rage,
These machines can tell you what to do,
If we try to live like this,
Things are going to be a mess,
I think my GPS is confused.

J Holt 5-2-08

The Animal Trainer

Carnal, it seemed, was a genius,
He trained a dangerous beast,
He made it perform for the public,
Who thought wonders, never would cease.

He dressed up the beast to look human,
It mimicked the actions of man,
The beast went through all the motions,
Though trained, it could not understand.

Today we must bury poor Carnal,
The guilty beast, feeling no pain,
The treats for the training never erased,
The beast instinct born in its brain.

Man cannot humanize animals,
To do so would desecrate God,
Carnal forever will speak of this truth,
From six feet under the sod.

J Holt 9-10-10

A Well Spent Yesterday

Wisdom spoke amid the roar,
I listened and I learned much more,
    Than those who talked.
Fretful sped from place to place,
Seeing naught that left a trace,
    I saw much more because I walked.

Doubt demands a full report
Before endeavor he supports,
    I let God plan.
Self implies that God include
His own thoughts and attitudes,
    I do not have to understand.

Pride refused the needed pain,
A necessary part of change,
    I went God's way.
Slothful, looking through Life's door,
Only craved, but did no more,
    I reap a well spent yesterday.

J Holt 12-19-09

The Good Old Days

The burdens of life will weigh heavy
On one who cuddles the past,
And cannot let go of the garish show,
And struggles to make it last.

The far-away scenes in the memory,
Are splendid when viewed in the mind,
Proverbial birds of paradise,
Their plumage improves with time.

We think of our yore, the things we adore,
And give them a smiling nod,
The die has been cast for things of the past,
But not for our meeting with God.

We don't find it hard to be our own bard,
Recalling the deeds we have done,
Subtle the blinding of memories still binding,
With more life yet to be run.

Good memories are sweet and consoling,
Some bad ones never will budge,
The past of old deeds won't meet final needs,
When each one must answer the Judge.

Innocent, harmless things of the past,
Enhanced to mean too much,
Can render one blind to life defined,
And keep one far out of touch.

An outstanding past accomplishment,
Can give one a "place" in the clan,
But visiting again and again the occasion,
A merry-go-round with no plan.

Memories are sweetest possessions,
They flavor the life of today,
But yesterday is a thing of the past,
And that is where it will stay.

J Holt 4-19-13

The Dour Gang

Dour and Sour were outlaws,
Terrorizing small towns,
Robbing all of positive thinking,
And many sheriffs gunned down.

Quietly, they rode into Peaceful,
Just as the sun finished day,
They stopped in front of the Long-Branch,
And went in their usual way.

The townspeople trembled to see them,
These citizens lived by the law,
Their guns carried many more notches,
Than those who were slow on the draw.

The sheriff of Peaceful told Dour,
"Saddle up now and leave town,
Our hearts and lives are in Peaceful,
We won't have your kind hanging round."

Dour had two deadly pistols,
The sheriff, a Colt forty-four,
The people cheered when all the smoke cleared,
For Dour lay dead on the floor.

There's dancing tonight on the prairie,
There's joy in this small western town,
The people are free to think once again,
Since Dour was finally gunned down.

J Holt 5-19-07

The Winepress

Two saints walked the road of life,
Each one gladly bore the strife,
And neither seemed to be depressed,
Until they came to God's winepress.

There was no path that lead aside,
They were confined to so abide,
God must crush His saints in time,
For grapes don't volunteer their wine.

The wheels of Providence are strong,
One yielded gall, the other song,
The yielded saint's love was not wasted,
Refreshing weary ones who tasted.

J Holt 12-17-12

Redneck

Redneck won the lottery
   And told it all around,
He'd had enough of country life,
   He's moving into town,
He shed his old blue coveralls
   And dressed himself up sharp,
He brought along his best coon dogs,
   And put them in the yard.

He joined up at the country club,
   But found out all too soon,
The place, though quite impressive,
   Did not have spittoons,
The more he learned, the more he knew
   His high-class hopes would sink,
He found he could not mingle well,
   Where pastimes were to think.

All too soon successful life
   For Redneck, lost its thrill,
He missed his old blue coveralls,
   And grinding at the mill,
His lottery wealth is gone now,
   It seemed but a mirage,
And Redneck raised coon dogs
   In his double car garage.

J Holt 1-22-98

Contemplation

Hesitate was a thinking man
    Deep in contemplation,
His greatest joy was time he spent
    Reflecting on reflection,
Deep thought fascinated him and
    Charmed him by the hour,
He was entertained but never
    Used his thinking power.

He wrestled with the deeper thoughts
    Of life that mystify,
He bathed in warm philosophies that
    Left him satisfied,
His mind ascended up until the
    Altitude restrained,
His thoughts and ideas were his toys,
    His playground was his brain.

J Holt 5-10-97

Beggar or Boss

He asked more of Life than existed,
Ruthless with those who would serve,
Scorned all the bounty Heaven could offer,
For better he though he deserved.

He scolded all people, demanding,
He lived, a covert parasite,
Ruling with iron hand of volunteer service,
Pretending it was his delight.

He practiced pretended submission,
So meek as his subtle façade,
He mastered the art of excuses,
Refusing his acre of sod.

Those who thoughtlessly ventured
Too close to his social embrace,
Would find in due time their fiber of mind
With his own completely replaced.

He treads light with kind, friendly gestures,
Cloaking the true man, uncouth,
He guards his facade, for it is his god,
And passes it off as the truth.

Life had refused his excuses,
Demanding full measure of cost,
He loathed to be helpless as beggar,
When Life had refused him as boss.

J Holt 7-14-07

The Candle

I took a piece of candle
   From the holder where it burned,
And placed it near the flame
   And watched it melt and I discerned.

Fire is fire and purifies
   Wherever given space,
Like burning fire, the Holy Truth,
   Will never yield its place.

The smaller flame does not impress
   Those craving power and worth,
But smaller fires truly power
   The engines of the earth.

Surface understanding can
   Easily float away,
On the tide of ignorance common
   With the learned ones today.

Geniuses conceive their thoughts,
   And engineers their plans,
But great ideas remain ideas,
   Without the common man.

J Holt 10-31-13

Weffa

(When our granddaughter Aletha was born, her sister Mareta was barely two. She could not say Aletha, she called her Weffa. We, as grandparents thought it cute and used it ourselves.)

When God started weaving the cloth of my life,
And decided just how it would be,
Carefully He wove in the threads of His choosing,
And one of those threads was thee,
He wove in some rain and some rainbows,
Some flowers, for beauty, you see,
He wove in a bright, sparkling sunbeam,
We called her Weffa Wee.

J Holt 7-25

ABOUT THE AUTHOR

John Holt grew up a county boy, the sixth child of ten. His family attended a small Baptist Church that needed a congregational song leader when John was fourteen. This was the start of his involvement in music, that was to last more than fifty-five years.

John, and his wife Lon Nell, are graduates of Arlington Baptist College where he studied music and was the featured soloist in Handel's Messiah, the Opera Il Trovatore and other major productions.

They live near Columbus, Ohio and have been married fifty-seven years, have three children, twelve grandchildren, and eleven great grandchildren.

John is still busy in music, is an experienced beekeeper, and a craftsman building special desks and bookcases for his special-needs grandson Toby.

John's previous book, DANNY'S WORLD, is available in paperback and Kindle editions at Amazon.com and in audio form at audible.com. Future books coming soon are Books 2 and 3 of his POEMS THAT MATTER Poetry Series, and two nonfiction releases; HAVE A GOOD DAY – EVEN IF IT TAKES ALL DAY, and FRIEND TRAFFICKING, both to be published on Amazon.com.

John Holt   Poems That Matter – Book One

Alphabetical Listing of Poems – Book 1

A Candle...73
A Gentle June Rain...31
A Hug Would Make My Day...70
A Philosophical View of...94
A Well Spent Yesterday...129
Afterglow of A Hug...45
Again!...81
An Inch of Time...120
An Organized Mind...118
Approval... 46
As A Man Thinketh...62
As the Child Is Bent...102
Autonomy...47
Bad Apples...58
Beauty...49
Bringing Home The Bacon...29
Busy...34
Contemplation...135
Beggar or Boss...136
Daddies...54
Deadly Faults...87
Death of A Snowflake...90
Defrauded...15
Destiny...23
Disadvantage is Advantage...80
Don't Sweat the Small Stuff...81
Essie and Effie...103
Eternal Worth...35
Faith and Intellect...108
False Guilt...85
Family Reunion Memories...37
Farewell To The Lazy...48
First Thoughts...109
Funny Barnyard Scene...47
God Set A Time...112
Good Medicine...86
Growing Up...70
Habits...122
The Unknown Trail...123
Significance...124
Materialism...125
This Newfangled Electronic Age...126
The Animal Trainer...128
Heartaches...105
Hilda the Cook...57
Home...119
How To Succeed...65
Hug Me!... 60
I Wear A Smile...76

I'd Rather Draw the Blueprints...16
If You Faint in The Day of Adversity...82
If You Will Try...104
Impossible Things...18
In A Tizzy...77
Irritation...91
The Mantle of The Day...92
Klausen And Boone...14
Lacing My Shoes...50
Laughter...20
Letting Go...59
Look Beyond the Trees...66
Loyalty...61
Mining The Heart...53
My Guinea Pig Ted...99
Never Give Gifts...111
Ode to Ego...109
Ode to The Fisherman...39
Ode to The Omelet Maker...74
Ode to The Poet Carpenter...115
Old Mose...90
Old Parents...60
One Small Rose...114
Pearls Before Swine...101
Raindrops...27
Reaching Higher...63
Redneck...134
Rejection...113
Robin Hood...98
Rowing Against the Tide...84
Secluded Island...88
Shout Is Clout to The Dumb...46
Simple Gifts...48
Situational Ethics...61
Small Men...60
Spring Shelter...32
Springtime in Texas...64
Success...72
Sunshine for The Children...33
Sunshine For The Heart...68
Talk Is Cheap...93
The All-American Pig...96
The Anvil...97
The Athlete Lee...95
The Bond of The Heart...83
The Butterfly...75
The Candle...138

John Holt					Poems That Matter – Book One

The Daily Fray...42
Procrastination...43
The Brutish Man...44
The Diamond...106
The Dictator...26
The Dour Gang...132
The End Is the Beginning...56
The Fat Man...65
The Fool and The Fireplace...74
The Good Old Days...130
The Heart Song...69
The Kids Are Gone, But----51
The Land Of Fantasy...38
The Land Of Lying...71
The Life House...85
The Lonely Man of Contention...40
The Make Up of The Day...52
The Manipulator...24
The Mongrel Millionaire...78
The Obviation of Buford Jones...113
The Optimist...55
The Parachutist...32
The Parasite...25
The Pendulum Swings Where...116
The Pioneer Man...105

The Purpose Of A Poem...67
The Security of The Familiar...99
The Shortest Way Home...110
The Skeptic And The Feather...28
The Sour Man...22
The Toothpick...75
The Uncommon Common Man...112
The Winepress...133
The Wordsmith...119
Thinker...100
Time II...121
Time Passes So Fast...64
To lighten up the Load...101
Urgency of Goals...100
Wasted Life...14
Watching The Clock...30
Water Seeks Its Level...121
Weffa...139
Why Do We Do It?...36
Worry...34
Ode To The Stone Caster...35
Wretched...79
You Never Will Know...95

Alphabetical Listing by First Line

A candle keeps you company - 73
A far-sighted snake named old Mose, - 90
A gentle jeweler happened on a - 106
A hug gives something to one - 86
A man's a fool to change the rules, - 63
A shivering man came - 74
A skeptic thought a feather was - 28
A small rose bloomed by the - 114
A warm contentment lingers - 45
An organized mind is a good sign, - 118
An understanding pioneer man - 105
At first his words were soft and - 24
Beauty confined in timed sound - 49
Buried deep in the heart of my - 69
Carnal, it seemed, was a genius, - 128
Cast not your pearls before the - 101
Daddies are fathers who've grad - 54
Dour and Sour were outlaws, - 132
Essie and Effie were sisters, - 103
Experience travels with Provide - 110
Faith and intellect will fight - 108
Few are the men craving honest - 94
Flowers bloomed by the old board - 64
Generally, the man who rows the - 61
Give me the man who'll do the - 72
God set a season when - 112
God will give enough heartaches - 105
Habits which we form in youth, - 122
Hay-Cuh-Luh-Cay-Cuh, the man - 115
He asked more of Life than exist - 136
He gave deep thought to what he - 101
He has a pot belly that wobbles - 96
He leaned on the hoe and looked - 124
He yelled and screamed and yet - 22
Here lie the bones of Hilda the - 57
Here lie the bones of my guinea - 99
Hesitate was a thinking man - 135
I ain't skeered that Ah mite fell, - 113
I can do it myself Dad, - 70
I have an itch I cannot reach - 91
I knew I was loved by my mom - 50
I love the busy life, I do, - 34
I saw a poor man near the street, - 15
I suppose there's nothing else - 85
I took a piece of candle - 138
I waited for this Robin Hood - 98
I want to introduce you to - 78
I was in my car one day - 126
I wear the same smile everyday - 76
I will make all your decisions, - 26
I would give my millions - 120
I'd rather draw the blueprints - 16
I'd rather have the sunshine - 48
I'm a simple wordsmith, - 119
I've found a quiet secluded isle, - 88
I've heard it said by sages - 83
I've heard people say that it never- 116
I've laughed away a ton of care - 20
If I am to bring home the bacon, - 29
If the sun shines on the flowers - 33
If the sun shines on the flowers, - 68
If trees find their ample water - 82
If we could get enough of the - 125
If we gathered up the minutes - 14
If you want a close look - 75
Into the land of fantasy - 38
It seemed to be a tragic death, - 90
It's hard to explain why we suffer - 46
Just for today I'll try to do more, - 63
Keep your spirit up and you win! - 81
Klausen and Boone were railroad - 14
Life in the land of lying, - 71
Life is like an unknown trail, - 123
Like dripping unending of water - 40
Never give gifts without reason, - 111
On distant plains of destiny, - 23
One hundred sixty-eight hours are - 64
One of the hardest, things parents - 59
Raindrops ever falling ever - 27
Redneck won the lottery - 134
Small is the man who thinks he is - 60
So often the role of the parent - 60
Someone has said that you can't - 66
Something marvelously wonderful - 70
Sometimes when you think you are- 56
Stay on the job where you're - 39
That which totally devastates - 113
The anvil will outlast the hammer, - 97
The brutish man, when young and - 44
The burdens of life will weigh - 130
The cloth of our soul that we wear - 42
One of his self-deceptions, - 43
The earth would be rid of the lazy, - 48
The first thoughts of the day - 109
The first thoughts of the day - 92
The folks who sweat the small - 81
The greatest of all men among us - 112
The life that you live will be empty - 30
The long limber branches - 32
The man who talks of noble things - 93

John Holt   Poems That Matter – Book One

The miniature shoes on the dress - 51
The night must come with cloak - 80
The old heifer sneezed, and fell - 47
The only worthwhile way to spend - 35
The optimist sees the acorn, - 55
The purpose of a poem is to - 67
The smell of hay rich in my face, - 31
The soft touch of my tendrils is - 25
The thing that stops the average man- 99
The things in life that really bug us, - 60
The timid man waits on the shore - 84
The toothpick is a curious stick, - 75
The vintage saying is that "One - 58
The words we said were very few, - 52
There are no houses ever built - 85
There is a deadly thing we do, - 87
There is a fire that burns inside a - 100
There is a good omelet maker Jim, - 74
There is a heart treasure hidden, - 53
There once was a man from Perth, - 65
There once was a parachutist - 32

There once was a stone caster Walt, -
35ere once was an athlete Lee, - 95
They shape and mold the spirit, - 102
Thinker longed to find secrets - 100
To say 'I remember' is saying I've - 37
Two saints walked the road of - 133
Water seeks its level, - 121
We go in debt to dress ourselves - 36
What you think is what you are, - 62
When day is dark, I rest my heart, - 119
When God started weaving the - 139
When we're busy in a tizzy, - 77
Whether or not you raise your voice 46
Wisdom spoke amid the roar, - 129
Worry will not empty out tomorrow - 34
Wretched committed a horrible crime- 79
Yesterday will not return, - 121
You cannot drink yourself sober, - 18
You could have a purpose - 104
You need not be a genius, - 65
You never will know what you're - 95